Sweet Spa!

by
Jenna Land Free

Pamper Party

It can be hard to take care of your hair and skin, especially when you have to buy beauty products. Most store-bought spa stuff contains a lot of chemicals. That's one reason it's better to create spa treats at home. Saving your allowance is another!

The All-Natural Spa Lab will teach you how to use natural ingredients to make store-quality beauty products yourself. All you need are the tools in this kit, some basic items from around the house, and an adult to help you.

Soon you'll be pampering yourself with a relaxing bath or a refreshing facial, but first you'll need to measure, sprinkle, stir, and experiment in your kitchen spa lab!

you'll make...
⚙ a scrub out of brown sugar
⚙ a face mask out of avocado
⚙ a skin cleanser out of a grape

you'll learn...
the secrets behind many super-powered ingredients, including how to use baking soda for reasons that have nothing to do with baking.

you'll use...
⚙ molds to make bath bombs
⚙ glitter in your lip gloss

you'll experiment...
with extra ingredients whenever you see the "Creative Juice" flower. Give them a try or come up with your own ideas!

Creative Juice!

Spa Menu

Bath-bombs
Basic
Minty Me
Kool-Aid Pool
Nuts About Bath-Bombs
Chocolate Heaven
Wrap it Up
Tri-color Pop

Scented Stones

Face Masks
Lemon & Egg
Egg & Honey
Oatmeal Exfoliator
Avocado
Grape Cleanser

Fruit Smoothie Hair Mask

Bath Time
Milk & Honey Bath Oil
Fizzy Bath Salts
Tea Bath
Floral Tea Bath

Body Scrubs
Oatmeal Sugar
Brown Sugar & Lemon
Sugar

Fairy Dust

Fairy Glitter Gel

Lip Balms
Basic
Chocolate
Vanilla
Berry
Lipstick recycle

100 years ago in London, England, women didn't want anyone to know they used beauty products. There was a famous salon called the House of Cyclax. Its customers would wear veils and sneak in the back, so they could keep their secret _secret_.

Heads Up!!

A lot of your spa products will look and smell delicious. But don't eat them! They'll taste gross, and then you won't be able to use them on your skin and hair. For hungry experimenters, it's a good idea to have a tasty snack nearby so you won't be tempted.

The ingredients in the following recipes are all-natural, but you still might be allergic or sensitive to them. If your skin turns red or blotchy from using any of these products, stop!

Equipped to Relax

Choose your own spa adventure! Mix and match the equipment in your kit to make your own special combinations. Start with the recipes in this book, but don't stop there.

Be sure to wash your equipment before and after each project.

Stir Spoons

Mix, fold, mash, and dish up some beauty using these stir spoons. Use the small end to mix things in the small lidded pots. use the large end in the large pots.

Molds

Sweets in the bathtub? Not exactly. But you can make bath-bombs in the shape of a cupcake, popsicle, or piece of candy. You can also use the molds to make scented stones for your dresser drawers.

Large Lidded Pots

Perfect for mixing! Or use them to store your body scrubs. Leave them in the bathroom so they're ready to go when you are.

Citric Acid

Your kit comes with enough citric acid for four projects. You can purchase more at any specialty grocery store. Each packet contains 20 grams or approximately 2 tablespoons.

Don't be fooled by the chemical-sounding name. Citric acid comes from citrus fruits like lemons and limes. It's what puts the fizz in your bath-bombs and bath salts.

Small Lidded Pots

Use these dainty pots to hold glitter gel and lip balm. They're small enough to fit into your pocket or purse.

Glitter

Share the shine! Sprinkle glitter in your bath molds, lip gloss, and fairy dust. Use a little or use a lot!

Pamper Pantry

Here are tools and ingredients you'll need from around the house:

- Measuring spoons
- Measuring cups
- Paper towels
- Microwaveable bowl
- Microwave oven
- Knife
- Rolling pin or cylindrical can
- Cutting board
- Blender
- Saucepan
- Cookie cutters
- Fork
- Coffee filter
- Cotton balls
- Ribbon
- Scissors
- Cheesecloth

Check out each recipe before you get started. You may need some of these items, too:

- Oatmeal or oat flour
- Honey
- Baking soda/bicarbonate of soda
- Cornstarch
- Flour
- Salt/Sea salt
- Shortening
- Eggs
- Water
- Brown sugar
- Cinnamon
- Ginger
- Cocoa powder
- Drink crystals
- Chocolate chips
- Lemon juice
- Plain yogurt
- Banana
- Apple
- Avocado
- Grape
- Herbal tea
- Coconut milk
- Almond oil
- Olive oil
- Vegetable oil
- Essential oils
- Flavored extracts
- Food coloring
- Flower petals
- Aloe vera gel
- Petroleum jelly
- Baby powder

Bomb Shell

Toss this bath-bomb into a warm tub to see it fizz and foam. Step in and feel the water tingle and tickle you. After soaking, you'll smell so good you'll never want to get dirty again!

Bath-Bomb Basic

NATURAL NEEDS

- Cooking oil: olive or vegetable
- Glitter (optional)
- 1/4 cup (60g) baking soda/bicarbonate of soda
- 2 tablespoons cornstarch
- 1 packet (20g) citric acid
- 1/2 tablespoon water for sprinkling

SPA SETUP

- Measuring spoons and cups
- Paper towel
- Mold—cupcake, popsicle, or candy
- Bowl
- Stir spoon

Step One

- Pour a dab of cooking oil onto your paper towel. Rub it around inside both halves of the mold.

- Sprinkle glitter over the oil, if you like. As little or as much as you want.

Step Two

- Measure baking soda, cornstarch, and citric acid into your bowl.
- Mix with stir spoon.

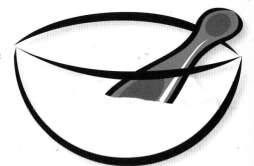

NOTE:
The slippery oil will make it easier to remove the bath-bomb from the mold when it's time

Step Three

* Measure out the water into a small bowl.
* Flick the water onto the mixture a few times.

> NOTE:
> Flicking is all in the fingers! When your hand is wet, close your fingers to make a fist, then open them up quickly. A handmade sprinkler system!

* Mix the water in with your hands. It should feel dry but still stick together.
* Take a handful of the mixture and squeeze your hand into a fist.

> NOTE:
> If it sticks together, move on to step four. If not, flick some more water onto it and mix until it does hold a shape. You may not need to use all of the water.

Step Four

* A handful at a time, fill each half of the mold to overflowing. Pack it down.
* If you use the candy mold, skip to step five now.

> If you're using the popsicle or cupcake mold, sprinkle a little water on each side. It should fizz a little.

> Use a stir stick as a handle for your popsicle bath-bomb!

* Carefully snap the sides together.

Step Five

* Leave the mixture in the mold for 20 minutes.
* Carefully take out the bath-bomb. Let it dry overnight.

Step Six

* When you want to use your bath-bomb, run some warm water into a bathtub and drop it in.
* Watch it fizz! Then enjoy a bath you made out of all-natural ingredients.
* Once you've become a bath-bomb expert, try one of the variations on pages 8 - 9!

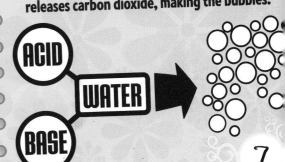

Fizz-icist!

What made your calm bath fizz like a soda pop? The reaction of an acid (the citric acid) and a base (the baking soda/bicarbonate of soda). They live together in the bath-bomb but stay separate until you add water. The water makes them react to each other which releases carbon dioxide, making the bubbles.

ACID + BASE → WATER →

Creative Juice!

Once you know how to make a basic bath-bomb, you can experiment with different colors and smells. Try one of these. Just add in the extra ingredients between step two and step three in the Bath-Bomb Basic recipe.

Minty Me

The festive colors make it a good Christmas present.

Add 1/8 teaspoon peppermint extract to make it smell fresh.

Add 3 drops of green or red food coloring to make it look minty.

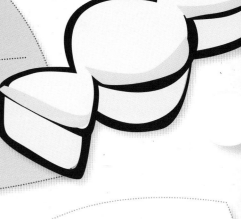

Nuts about Bath-Bombs

Add 1/8 teaspoon almond extract.

Add 3 drops of brown or orange food coloring to go with the nutty almond smell.

Or use blue, red, or green to throw people off the scent.

Kool-Aid Pool

Ever felt like splashing around in a pool of Kool-Aid?

Add 1/2 teaspoon Kool-Aid or other drink crystals.

Chocolate Heaven

Bathing in chocolate doesn't need to be just a dream!

Add 1/2 teaspoon cocoa powder.

It may look like watery mud, but your bath will smell so good you'll want to wash it down with a glass of milk!

Wrap it Up

Make this cupcake look real enough to eat.

Divide your mixture into two parts.

Add 3 drops of food coloring into each part.

Keep them separate when you follow step three.

Pack one color for the frosting; pack the other for the wrapper.

Tri-color Pop

No need to chase the ice cream truck. Make your own tricolored popsicle!

Divide your mixture into three parts.

Add 3 drops of food coloring into each part.

Keep them separate when you follow step three.

Pack them into your mold in three short stripes.

Miracle Material!

Citric acid doesn't look (or sound) like much, but there's huge talent in the little powder. Besides reacting in your bath-bomb, it also acts as a natural preservative (PRIH-zerv-uh-tiv). That means it keeps foods from spoiling.

Try this:

Get two apple slices.
Squeeze lemon juice on one.
Leave the other alone.
Let them sit for 15 minutes.
Compare the two slices.

FINDINGS:
Citric acid kept the inside of the apple looking nice and fresh, because lemons have citric acid in them. Citric acid is found in oranges and other citrus fruits, too.

9

Sense of Calm

Smelly socks, be gone! Banish stink for good! Just make scented stones and toss them into your sock and pajama drawers. They'll last for months, and you'll smell so fresh all day!

Brain Wave

You know how when you smell cinnamon rolls, you get hungry? What's happening is your nose is sending a message to a part of your brain that makes you feel like eating. Many people believe fragrance oils or "essential oils"—which are taken from plants—work the same way. It's called "aromatherapy."

Aroma Chart!

I SMELL...	I FEEL...
Lavender	Calm and Relaxed
Spicy or citrus oil	Energetic

Does aromatherapy really work? Well, it smells nice, and who can argue with that?

Scented Stones

NATURAL NEEDS

- 3/4 cup + 2 tablespoons (112g) flour
- 2 tablespoons salt
- 1/8 teaspoon cornstarch
- 1/3 cup (80 ml) water
- 1 teaspoon fragrance extract or 16 drops essential oil
- 3 drops food coloring

SPA SETUP

- Measuring spoons and cups
- An adult
- 2 bowls (1 that is microwave-safe)
- Microwave oven
- Stir spoon
- Rolling pin or cylindrical can or container
- Cookie cutters or mold— popsicle, candy, or cupcake (optional)

Step One

🐾 Measure flour into a bowl.

🐾 Add salt and cornstarch. Mix with your stir spoon.

Step Three

🐾 Stir water mixture into dry mixture.

🐾 Knead it with your hands until a lot of the dry ingredients are blended in. It should feel like cookie dough.

🐾 Too sticky for you? Add more flour.

Step Two

🐾 With an adult's help, heat water in the microwave for 40 seconds.

🐾 Stir into the water a favorite smell, from a flavored extract or essential oil.

🐾 Add food coloring. Use any color you want, but dark colors look best.

Step Four

🐾 Roll out mixture to about 1/4-inch (.6 cm) thick.

🐾 Cut shapes using cookie cutters. Or roll your mixture into a ball, like a river rock.

🐾 Let dry overnight.

Creative Juice!

Try packing your mixture into one of your molds to shape it. Just don't forget to remove it! Adding oil and a dusting of flour to the mold before you start can help.

The French went wild for perfumes in the 18th century. In King Louis XV's court, everything smelled as pretty as it looked. Scent was added to skin, clothes, fans, and furniture. Sofas never had it so good before...or since!

Super-ingredient alert!

Cornstarch might not look like the yellow kernel it comes from, but don't let that fool you. It does come from corn, and it's used as a "binder," something that helps ingredients stick together.

Cornstarch is used in a ton of the products we use every day. like baby powder, pudding, and powdered sugar. It helps thicken sauces and soups, too. You'll never look at corn on the cob the same way again!

scrub-a-dub

Body scrubs feel rough when you use them, but it's worth it when you rinse off. They make your skin soft and moist. Use your scrubs in the bath, but don't put any on your face.

Spa Plan
You only have two large lidded pots, so don't make these all at once. Store them until you're ready to scrub.

Oatmeal Sugar Scrub

NATURAL NEEDS

- 3 tablespoons brown sugar
- 2 tablespoons oat flour (or ground oatmeal)
- 1 tablespoon honey
- 2-3 tablespoons olive oil
- 1/8 teaspoon flavored extract or essential oil (optional)

SPA SETUP

- Measuring spoons and cups
- Bowl
- Stir spoon
- Large lidded pot

Step One

- Mix the brown sugar and oat flour (or ground oatmeal) together in your bowl.
- Add the honey.
- Drizzle the olive oil over the mixture.

Step Two

- Add flavored extract or essential oil, if you want. Vanilla works well!

Step Three

- Use your stir spoon to combine ingredients well.
- When the mix sinks to the bottom of the bowl and the oil rises to the top, you're done!
- Spoon into pot!

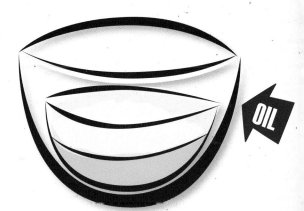

OIL

Brown Sugar and Lemon Scrub

Sugar Scrub

NATURAL NEEDS

- 2-3 tablespoons olive oil
- 1/2 teaspoon flavored extract or essential oil
- 1/4 cup + 2 tablespoons (75g) brown sugar, packed

SPA SETUP

- Measuring spoons and cups
- Bowl
- Stir spoon
- Large lidded pot

Step One

🐾 Mix oil and flavored extract or essential oil together in a bowl.

Step Two

🐾 Add the brown sugar and mix in well. Spoon into pot!

NATURAL NEEDS

- 1/2 cup (110g) brown sugar
- 1/2 cup (120g) salt
- 1 tablespoon lemon juice
- 1 tablespoon almond oil
- 1 tablespoon honey

SPA SETUP

- Bowl
- Stir spoon
- Large lidded pot

Step One

🐾 Mix brown sugar and salt in bowl.

Step Two

🐾 Add the lemon juice, almond oil, and honey, and mix well.

🐾 Spoon into pot.

Miracle Material

Olive oil is another super-powered ingredient! It's full of vitamins A and E, which may help protect skin from sun harm.

Try this:

RUB IT ON YOUR HANDS.
SOAK YOUR NAILS IN IT.
RUB IT ON YOUR LIPS.

WHAT DID YOU DISCOVER?

Olive oil makes your hands softer, and your nails stronger, and keeps your lips from chapping. Just don't try to pick anything up afterwards, because it'll slip right out of your hands!

13

Glitter and Shine

Have you ever noticed someone whose face seems like it has a special sparkle straight from the sun? Probably it's just a little science and creativity, held together with honey—or maybe even cornstarch! Here's how you can get special sun rays, too.

Fairy Dust

NATURAL NEEDS

* 1 teaspoon baking soda/bicarbonate of soda
* 1 teaspoon cornstarch
* 1 teaspoon baby powder or regular dusting powder
* Glitter

SPA SETUP

* Measuring spoons
* Bowl
* Fork
* Coffee filter or piece of fabric
* 4 cotton balls
* Ribbon

Step One

* Measure out all ingredients into a bowl.
* Stir with a fork, mixing gently but thoroughly.

Step Two

* Poke three small holes in the center of a coffee filter or piece of fabric.
* Gently pour the dusting powder into a coffee filter.

Step Three

* Loosen the cotton balls and blend together to make one large cotton ball. Lay the cotton over the powder.

Step Four

* Tie the filter or piece of fabric with a ribbon to close.
* When you feel like it, pat some powder on your body for a little extra sparkle!

Baking Soda's Secret!

Baking soda is a chemical compound that's found in many mineral springs. (Have you ever seen a spring? It's a spot where water comes up through the earth, bringing a lot of minerals from rocks with it.)

Baking soda makes your fairy dust the perfect texture, and has a ton of other uses. It gets stinky smells out of books, helps upset stomachs, and whitens teeth.

Fairy Glitter Gel

NATURAL NEEDS
- ❋ Aloe vera gel
- ❋ Honey
- ❋ Glitter

SPA SETUP
- ❋ Stir spoon
- ❋ Small lidded pot

EASY BEING GREEN
If you have an aloe plant, you can find the clear gel directly in its leaves! Just break off a piece and squeeze out the gel.

Step One
- 🐾 Fill small lidded pot 3/4 full of aloe vera gel.

Step Two
- 🐾 Add a few drops of honey. Mix together.
- 🐾 Stir in the glitter.

Step Three
- 🐾 Use the glitter gel on your face or body to give yourself a little extra sparkle!

Aloe Vera
Aloe vera (AL-oh VER-uh) is used in lots of skin and beauty products, like cleansers, moisturizers, and creams. It has a reputation for soothing skin. The gel alone can be used to relieve skin irritations, like a sunburn.

Hidden Honey

Honey in makeup? Because it's so sticky (which is a pain when you want to get it out of the jar), honey is used in products that need a binder. Guess what else it's used in?

Start your own search for hidden honey. Read the ingredient labels on packaging. What other hidden ingredients can you find?

**SAUCES
SPREADS
LOTIONS
SOAPS**

**ROOT BEER
TEA
CEREAL
MEATS**

Try this:
Next time you have a sore throat, try some hot water with honey and lemon. The sticky honey coats your throat, making it feel better for a little while.

Pucker Up!

Once you learn the main recipe for lip balm, you can add whatever colors or flavors you'd like! Here are a few suggestions, and you can probably come up with even more on your own.

Be Gentle

This recipe uses petroleum jelly, which is natural, but some makers of beauty products use gentler ingredients like beeswax. You can use organic petroleum-free jelly and get the same results.

Lip Balm Basic

NATURAL NEEDS

- ❀ 2 teaspoons petroleum jelly
- ❀ 1/8 teaspoon honey
- ❀ 1/8 teaspoon vegetable shortening

SPA SETUP

- ❀ Measuring spoons
- ❀ An adult
- ❀ Microwaveable bowl
- ❀ Microwave
- ❀ Stir spoon
- ❀ Small lidded pot

Petro-Who!

"Petroleum jelly"—it's a mouthful to say, and sounds like something you should put in your car's gas tank to make it run. It has an oil base, so if you try mixing it with water, you'll be frustrated—it won't work! What WILL work is putting it on dry lips, because the oil helps soften the skin.

Step One
🐾 Measure out all ingredients in a microwaveable bowl. Mix them together.

Step Two
🐾 With an adult's help, microwave at high power for 20 seconds.

🐾 Stir, then repeat until fully melted.

Step Three
🐾 Spoon your mixture into your small lidded pot.

Step Four
🐾 Freeze for 15 minutes, or until solid. Then you can apply it on your lips!

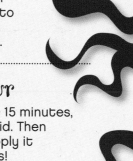

Chocolate

For dark and delicious lip balm:

🐾 Add 5 chocolate chips to the mixture before you put it in the microwave.

Don't add more than 5, though, or you'll look like you just ate a melted chocolate bar.

Vanilla

Smelling this lip balm will make you want to bake cookies!

🐾 Mix honey with 1/8 teaspoon of vanilla extract

🐾 Add the petroleum jelly and shortening.

🐾 Follow steps two, three, and four.

Creative Juice!

Here are some ideas for flavors and colors you can mix into your lip balm!

Berry

This lip balm tastes delicious, and has a pretty pink tint.

🐾 After step two, add 1/4 teaspoon berry-flavored drink crystals.

🐾 Then add 1-2 drops of water and mix. Keep stirring until the mixture thickens.

🐾 Now follow steps three and four.

Why add water? It makes the color of the drink crystals pop!

Lipstick Recycle

If you want a little more color to your lip balm, try this recipe:

🐾 Mix in some shavings of old lipstick before you microwave the mixture. This is after step one.

🐾 This is a great way to recycle the end of the tube, but be sure you get permission!

Oil and Water

In all of the recipes except the berry gloss, you add the extra ingredients BEFORE microwaving. But this won't work for the berry gloss. Why?

Because water and shortening or petroleum jelly won't mix together if they're cold! The reason? Water molecules are really attracted to one another, and oil (which is found in shortening) molecules are really attracted to one another. So neither water nor oil are interested in joining with the other. BUT when the oil gets heated, its molecules lose their love for each other. This gives the water molecules a chance to join in the fun.

17

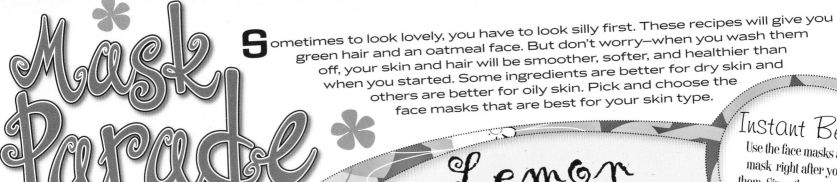

Mask Parade

Sometimes to look lovely, you have to look silly first. These recipes will give you green hair and an oatmeal face. But don't worry—when you wash them off, your skin and hair will be smoother, softer, and healthier than when you started. Some ingredients are better for dry skin and others are better for oily skin. Pick and choose the face masks that are best for your skin type.

Instant Beauty

Use the face masks and hair mask right after you make them. Since they include fresh ingredients, they won't last long enough to store.

Lemon & Egg Face Mask

The pore-tightening egg white in this recipe is great for normal to oily skin.

Heads Up!

Some people have sensitive skin. If yours turns red or blotchy from using any of these face masks, stop!

Eggs-actly!

HOW TO SEPARATE AN EGG:

Tap the center of your egg against a hard-edged bowl, so that it breaks. Take one half of the eggshell in each hand. The insides of the egg should be in one of the halves; the other half is empty. Hold both halves over the bowl. Carefully pour the yolk into the empty half, and let the whites spill into the bowl. This takes practice, so you might want to have a few eggs ready to go!

NATURAL NEEDS

* 1 egg white (Save the yolk! You'll use it in another recipe.)
* 1 tablespoon lemon juice

SPA SETUP

* Measuring spoons
* Bowl
* Fork
* Cotton ball

Step One

* Use a fork to beat the egg white until light and fluffy.

Step Two

* Gently fold and stir in the lemon juice.

Step Three

* Soak a cotton ball in the mixture, and apply to your face. It may make your face feel weird and tight.

* Leave it on for ten minutes. Then splash warm water on your face to rinse.

Egg & Honey Face Mask

NATURAL NEEDS

- 1 tablespoon honey
- 1 tablespoon plain yogurt
- 1 egg yolk (Did you save one from the Lemon & Egg Mask on page 18?)
- 1/2 teaspoon almond oil

SPA SETUP

- Measuring spoons
- Bowl
- Stir spoon

Dry to normal skin benefits from the rehydrating (ree-HI-dray-ting) ability of egg yolk. That means it adds moisture to your skin.

Step One

- Mix all of the ingredients together in a bowl.

Step Two

- Use your fingers to massage the mixture into your face and neck.
- Leave it on for 15 minutes, then gently rinse off with water.

Oatmeal Facial Exfoliator

Oatmeal absorbs dirt and gently exfoliates all skin types.

NATURAL NEEDS

- 2 heaping teaspoons oat flour (or ground oatmeal)
- 1 teaspoon baking soda/ bicarbonate of soda
- 1 teaspoon honey
- 1/2 teaspoon water

SPA SETUP

- Measuring spoons
- Bowl
- Stir spoon

Step One

- Combine oat flour (or ground oatmeal), baking soda, and honey, and mix well.

Step Two

- Add water. Mix to make a paste. If you need to add a little more water, that's okay! You want it to feel like mud.

Step Three

- Apply to your face with your fingers, and rub gently.
- Leave it on for 15 minutes, then rinse and gently pat dry.

Shed Like A Snake

Though you can't see it, your skin actually sheds every month. New skin is underneath the old, fresh and ready to go! Using an exfoliator (ex-FOH-lee-AY-ter) like this one just moves the shedding process along more quickly. It forces out the old and welcomes in the new.

19

Avocado Face Mask

All the vitamins and fatty acids in avocados help to smooth and moisturize all skin types, but it's best for dry to normal skin.

NATURAL NEEDS
* 1/2 ripe avocado (Use the other half for the Fruit Smoothie Hair Mask on page 21!)

SPA SETUP
* An adult
* Knife
* Bowl
* Stir spoon

How can you tell if an avocado is ripe? Ripe avocados have very dark, purplish-black outer skins. They should also be a little soft, but not mushy.

Step One
* With an adult's help, cut and open the avocado, remove the pit, and scoop out 1/2 of the meat.
* Mash the meat into a creamy texture. Get all of the clumps out!

Step Two
* Massage into your face and neck.
* Leave on for 15 minutes and gently rinse off.

All About Avocados!

Super-power Ingredient Alert!

· An avocado is packed with vitamins and healthy fats.
· It might not look like it, but an avocado is a fruit-not a vegetable.
· Some people call avocados "alligator pears," because their skin is tough and leathery.
· Once an avocado is cut open, its "meat" turns brown quickly. Any chance a little lemon juice might help?

Grape Cleanser

NATURAL NEEDS
* 1 grape

SPA SETUP
* Knife

Step One
* Cut a grape in half.
* Rub the inside of each half over your face.

Step Two
* Rinse your face. Did the grape cleanser make you feel cooler?

Grapes!
Grapes have antioxidants (an-tee-AWK-si-dents) in them. Antioxidants are molecules that may improve wrinkly and damaged skin.

20

Fruit Smoothie Hair Mask

NATURAL NEEDS

- 1/2 ripe banana
- 1/4 ripe avocado
- 1 tablespoon plain yogurt
- 1/2 cup (120 ml) coconut milk.

SPA SETUP

- An adult
- Cutting board
- Knife
- Measuring spoons and cups
- Blender
- Spoon

Step One

- Peel the banana, and tear off half. Eat the other half!
- With an adult's help, cut open the avocado, remove the pit, and scoop out 1/4 of the meat. (Or use leftovers from the Avocado Face Mask on page 20!)

Step Two

- Using a cutting board and a knife, chop all of the fruit into bite-sized pieces.

Step Three

- Toss your fruit into a blender, put on the lid, and turn on the blender. Keep it on until your mixture is smooth.

Step Four

- Massage into your hair and scalp.
- Leave hair mask on for 15 minutes, then rinse and shampoo.

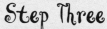

We suggest waiting until the next time you're going to take a bath or shower, otherwise your clothes are likely to get fruity and messy.

Scalp Appreciation!

We're really hard on our poor scalps. We pull and tug our hair from it, we scratch it when we're bored. Our scalp actually has a protective coating on it made of fats, but it gets hurt when we use a lot of shampoos. Enter banana! Bananas help the scalp get its fatty moisture back—which sounds gross, but it's actually really healthy!

21

Bath Attack

Soaking in a warm bath is a great way to relax. Especially if you're tired or cold. Use these bath mixes when you know no one will need to use the bathroom. You don't want to be interrupted. Relaxation takes time, after all!

Instant Beauty
Make these recipes right before you use them so you look good and they don't go bad!

Milk it!

This super-power ingredient probably isn't a surprise, since we're always told to drink milk. But why put it on your skin? Milk has been used as a natural skin cleanser for hundreds of years! It has lactic acid in it, which breaks up dead skin cells.

Milk also has vitamin A, a head-of-the-class vitamin that protects skin against infection and sun damage.

Milk & Honey Bath Salts

NATURAL NEEDS
* 1/2 cup (125ml) of milk (whole milk is best!)
* 1/4 cup (85g) honey
* 1 tablespoon baking soda/bicarbonate of soda
* 1/4 cup (60g) sea salt

SPA SETUP
* Measuring spoons
* Measuring cups
* Bowl
* Stir spoon

Step One
🐾 Combine milk, honey, baking soda, and salt in your bowl.

Step Two
🐾 Add to warm, running bath water.

Creative Juice!

Once you've added your mixture to your bath you can experiment! Try adding 2 tablespoons of baby oil to make your skin even softer. Or add a drop or two of your favorite essential oil. Breathe in the smell of relaxation.

Fizzy Bath Salts

NATURAL NEEDS
- 1/2 cup (115g) sea salt
- 1/3 cup (27g) baking soda/bicarbonate of soda
- 1 packet (20g) citric acid

- 5 drops of essential oil—pick your favorite!
- 5 drops of food coloring—what color do you feel today?

SPA SETUP
- Measuring cups
- Bowl
- Stir spoon

This recipe is made much like the bath-bomb basic on page 6. But you don't need to let it sit and harden. Instead, you can sprinkle it right into the tub. Use it when you need to relax in a hurry!

Step One
🐾 Mix ingredients together in bowl.

Step Two
🐾 Run your bath. Then sprinkle in your bath salts. Watch them fizz!

Tea Bath

NATURAL NEEDS
- 2 cups (480ml) water
- 4 teaspoons loose herbal tea—any kind you want!

SPA SETUP
- Measuring spoons
- Measuring cups
- An adult
- Pot for stovetop
- Strainer

Step One
🐾 With an adult's help, measure the water into a pot and boil it on the stovetop.

Step Two
🐾 Add the loose herbal tea to the water. Cover and turn the heat down to simmer.

Step Three
🐾 Leave it simmering for 10 minutes.

Step Four
🐾 With an adult's help, pour into a strainer over your bathwater. Breathe in and relax!

TEA BAG TRICK

Soaking in tea is as good as drinking it! Your skin soaks up the antioxidants and minerals that come from the tea. And it's relaxing. For a quick and easy way to help reduce puffy eyes.

TRY THIS:
- Run cold water over two tea bags.
- Place one on each eye.
- Rest for 10 minutes.
- Ah, refreshed!

23

Just One More...

Floral Tea Bath

NATURAL NEEDS

- ❁ Flower petals
- ❁ Water

SPA SETUP

- ❁ Scissors
- ❁ 10" x 10" doubled cheesecloth
- ❁ String or ribbon
- ❁ An adult
- ❁ Pot for stovetop

From a beautiful bouquet to a relaxing bath. But flowers aren't the only thing you can recycle. What other natural items can you think of to use in your own custom spa products?

Step One

- 🐾 Put the petals into your cut piece of cheesecloth.
- 🐾 Tie it with a string or ribbon.

Step Two

- 🐾 Put it in a pot of boiling water for 15 minutes.
- 🐾 Add the water to your bath. Voilà! You'll smell like a rose! Or a poppy, or a tulip, or whatever favorite flower is in bloom.

Sweet Spa!

© 2009 becker&mayer! LLC

Published by SmartLab®, an imprint of becker&mayer!

All rights reserved. SmartLab® is a registered trademark of becker&mayer! LLC, 11120 NE 33rd Place, Suite 101, Bellevue, Washington.

Creative development by Jim Becker and Aaron Tibbs

No part of this book may be reproduced, stored in a retrieval system, or transmitted in any form or by any means, electronic, mechanical, photocopying, recording, or otherwise, without the prior permission of SmartLab®. Requests for such permissions should be addressed to SmartLab® Permissions, becker&mayer!, 11120 NE 33rd Place, Suite 101, Bellevue, WA 98004.

If you have questions or comments about this product, please visit www.smartlabtoys.com/customerservice.html and click on the Customer Service Request Form.

Edited by Nancy Waddell · Written by Jenna Land Free

Package and book design by Eddee Helms

Design assistance by Steve Bodo

Illustrations by Ryan Hobson

Product photography by Keith Megay · SmartLab® character photography by Craig Harrold

Product development by Lauren Cavanaugh

Project and production management by Beth Lenz

Every effort has been made to correctly attribute all the material reproduced in this book. We will be happy to correct any errors in future editions.

Printed, manufactured, and assembled in Shenzhen China, June 2012

Sweet Spa! is part of the SmartLab® All-Natural Spa Lab kit.

Not to be sold separately.

ISBN-13: 978-1-60380-042-6

SL08837-11596